WHY YOUR MINISTRY FACEBOOK PAGE ISN'T WORKING

LET'S FIX IT!

JILL R. WALTZ

Why Your Ministry Facebook Page Isn't Working: Let's Fix It! © 2018 Jill Waltz

Published by Electric Moon Publishing, LLC
An author-friendly publishing place.
www.emoonpublishing.com
info@emoonpublishing.com

Paperback ISBN: 978-1-943027-25-5
E-book ISBN: 978-1-943027-26-2

Cover Design: Lyn Rayn, Electric Moon Publishing Creative Art Department

THE HOLY BIBLE, NEW INTERNATIONAL VERSION®, NIV® Copyright 1973, 1978, 1984, 2011 by Biblica, Inc.™ Used by permission. All rights reserved worldwide.

The Message. Copyright 1993, 1994, 1995, 1996, 2000, 2001, 2002. Used by permission of NavPress Publishing Group.

All rights reserved. No portion of this book may be reproduced, stored in a retrieval system, or transmitted in any form or by any means, except brief quotations in articles, reviews, or studies, without prior permission from the author. Contact Electric Moon Publishing, LLC for details.

Printed in the United States of America

www.emoonpublishing.com

"To fulfill our mission to make disciples of Jesus Christ in the nations, we need to go to where the people are. And people—more than two billion of them—are on Facebook. How can we engage outsiders in a natural, winsome, and loving manner, so that we might build bridges to Christ and the Church? Jill Waltz shares the why, the what, and the how behind using social media for effective ministry. This book is a valuable resource for anyone who cares about reaching people for Jesus in the modern world."

—**Rev. Albert Hung**, District Superintendent
Northern California Church of the Nazarene

"*Why Your Ministry Facebook Page Isn't Working: Let's Fix It!*, should be a must-read for everyone in ministry—especially those who are tasked with communication/outreach for their local congregation. The information Jill presents is clear and thorough. Her ability to explain technology in simple terms makes this book 'best-in-class' among those I have read on the subject. I would recommend all of our pastors read Jill's book."

—**Dr. Ron Blake**, District Superintendent
Indianapolis District Church of the Nazarene

Jill Waltz has provided a valuable resource for those of us who are needing two questions answered: "Would using Facebook benefit my church's ministry?" and "How do I set up and run a successful Facebook page for my church?" In this book, Jill employs her decades of experience of pastoral ministry as well as her successful venture establishing and running a lively Facebook page for ministers. You don't have to be a computer geek to read and use this book, as she clearly explains everything along the way and takes you through the steps to get your page up and running and keep it relevant and lively.

I recommend this book to all who seek to use social media to enhance the ministry of their congregation.

—**Dr. Ron Dalton**,
School of Theology and Christian Ministry
Olivet Nazarene University

Every pastor and church feels pressured to use social media. The problem is that social media can be a blessing or a curse. Simply using social media without a definitive plan will only create more problems and issues for a ministry. Waltz has crafted an excellent roadmap for those wanting to use social media effectively. This book is a must-read for those who want to remain relevant while engaging the world for Christ.

—**Carla Sunberg**,
General Superintendent, Church of the Nazarene

CONTENTS

Introduction	7
Part 1: Why Social Media?	11
1. Why Social Media?	13
2. The Question That Could Change Everything	19
3. Six Ways Social Media Sets the Table	23
Part 2: Getting Started	29
4. The What's, How's, and How Often to Post	31
5. Ten Tips to Develop Killer Posts That Increase Engagement	37
6. Becoming Multilingual (or Learning to Speak Facebook)	41
7. Design Hacks	45
8. Eleven of the Most Common Ministry Page Mistakes	49
9. Pages or Groups? Yes.	53
Part 3: Best Practices (Maintaining a Strong Presence)	59
10. Cutting Down on Content Chaos (Leveraging Tools to Master Content Management)	61
11. Three Tips to Gain Momentum	65
12. Using Video in Posts	73
13. Measuring Success	81
14. Building a Social Media Dream Team	85
Part 4: Ready-Made Content Ideas	89
15. Campaigns	91
16. 101 Conversation Starters	119
17. Fun Holidays/Events	125
18. Days of the Week Themes	129
Resources for Video or Inspirational News Clips	133
Endnotes	135

INTRODUCTION

In 2015, I was serving as a children's pastor in Anderson, Indiana. As any ministry leader does, I was constantly looking for ways to reach untapped markets of people. I took note of the fact that we didn't even have a Facebook page. I began to ask questions. Then, as if I needed one more thing to do in ministry, I blindly assumed the role of developing a social media ministry. You know how that goes in the church world, right? You say something as innocent as, "Hey, I think we need a social media presence. We seem to be missing a huge opportunity here." Next thing you know, you've got yourself a new ministry baby. And just as most parents feel overwhelmed and under-resourced when they're handed a new baby, I did, too. And yet, I was also naive enough to think I could turn my new baby into something beautiful and useful.

I knew we were missing the boat and I desperately wanted to catch up. I quickly discovered one of the most frustrating truths about working with social media: it is always evolving. Because of its organic nature, it is always growing. As with my other babies, as soon as I'd master one area of parenting, my kids had learned and conquered something new, requiring me to change my approach and game plan. Unlike other areas of ministry in which I spend time studying and mastering, social media is ever-changing. The organic nature of the medium is truly one of the hardest parts for me to embrace. I am a doer by nature. I like to make things happen, cross them off my list, then move on to the next item. I've had to learn to adjust my expectations when it comes to social media, ministry, and its usefulness within the church.

As I think back over now two decades of ministry, I can clearly see that the most rewarding seasons of ministry often came as the result of years of painstaking labor. Ministry with social media is no different. It moves fast, so you might expect fast results. If you're hoping for that sort of instant gratification, I'm afraid you'll quit in frustration six months from now. Plan to do the hard work, stay the course, and learn something new. I believe you'll see new ministry doors open if you do.

Learning to use social media won't instantly cause your church or ministry to explode overnight. What it will do, however, is provide you with opportunities to touch the lives of unchurched people in ways you never dreamed possible.

In many ways, social media ministry is being pioneered. Most of us really have no clue what to do or how to tame this out of control beast. I want to remind you that the pioneer life is difficult. It often isn't glamorous. But you'll have a sense of accomplishment at the end of the day. To know we've spread the message of Christ to people we've never had access to will motivate us to get up tomorrow and do the same thing. I'm challenged to put my eyes on the fact that lost people matter to Jesus. I'm motivated to use unconventional means to reach them. If you're up for an adventure, I invite you to hitch your wagon to mine as we pioneer a new land full of exciting promise together.

In Chapters 1-3, we will explore why your ministry needs to be investing in a quality Facebook page and how it will open new doors for your ministry. In Chapters 4-9, we'll talk about how you can add a social media ministry to your already existing ministry duties. In Chapters 10-14, we will get practical and talk about best practices. In the last portion, I offer practical suggestions to equip you to implement these ideas. I know you're busy, pastor. I know you're wearing a million hats. It is my hope that by doing some of the leg work for you, I will have provided you with months' worth of social media content ideas. I pray that God expands your table as a result.

WHAT SOCIAL MEDIA CAN DO FOR YOU

PART 1

WHY
SOCIAL MEDIA?

Communication has changed drastically over the past decade. From online marketing to 140-character nuggets of information, we've learned to communicate in new and exciting ways. This shift in communication has required churches to examine former methods and styles and make drastic course corrections. As cutting-edge platforms for communication are being developed, we must embrace this shift. In so doing, we multiply our efforts to be dealers of hope, reaching out to communities in current and exciting ways, and begin to understand the needs of those around us like never before.

Though social media provides countless advantages, here are my top six reasons that your church/ministry must have a social media presence:

1. **Connection.** Using social media allows you to establish a familiar face among people in your community you may not normally meet. It also allows you to connect with people in your community by breaking down the "walls" that often exist before someone ever physically enters your building. You might also be surprised to learn that social media fosters a deeper sense of community among your current congregation. And finally, discipleship is possible through the use of social media.
2. **You instantly become more relatable.** Showing yourself as a church and as individuals will help people realize that they're more like you than they may think. Many unchurched people have preconceived notions about what people within the church are like. Many times, those notions are wrong. Because of this when a person sees your ministry as relatable, you instantly gain a bit of credibility.
3. **Promotion.** With so many people on social media, why would you not use it to promote your church? (Don't make the mistake that a lot of churches make in using social media only for promotion—that's a big mistake.) If you're taking the time to read this book, I assume you have some exciting things happening within your ministry and you'd love to share them. There has never been such a time in history when advertising has been so easy and virtually free.
4. **Credibility.** Long before people visit restaurants or any sort of business, they check them out on social media. Ratings and reviews say so much about your

church or ministry and go a long way in helping establish the fact that you are credible, you care about people, and that you have a visible presence within your community—one that makes a difference.

5. **Website traffic growth.** Getting people to visit your church website is a big win. Giving them the opportunity to explore your church further (on their own turf and terms) is powerful. Ultimately, this is the final step most people will take in checking out a new ministry online. They often start with social media, where they will scroll through pictures and posts and read a few reviews, then they will move on to your website if they want to learn more.

6. **Outreach.** Social media is an often untapped mission field for churches. If our churches aren't there, they are missing out on an important opportunity to share the love of Christ with our communities.

So what's keeping you from developing a strong social media presence?

Time

Pastors and ministry leaders wear too many hats. But what if you could learn to leverage social media in a way that doesn't cost you hours per week? It is possible to develop a quality social media ministry without spending a lot of time on it. Stick around. We will chat about that.

Fear

Are you afraid of what people will say or do on your page? Afraid you won't be able to maintain posting? Well, stop living in fear. The truth is, sharing your faith is always risky. Learning something new is scary. Exposing yourself to controversy and conflict will make you feel vulnerable. By turning fear and insecurity into a boldness to share Christ, we can become like the apostle Paul who, because of the transformation Jesus made in his life, was willing to share the message using unconventional means and methods.

> I have voluntarily become a servant to any and all in order to reach a wide range of people: religious, nonreligious, meticulous moralists, loose-living immoralists, the defeated, the demoralized—whoever. I didn't take on their way of life. I kept my bearings in Christ—but I entered their world and tried to experience things from their point of view. I've become just about every sort of servant there is in my attempts to lead those I meet into a God-saved life. I did all this because of the Message. I didn't just want to talk about it; I wanted to be in on it! (1 Corinthians 9:19-23)

Fair Warning

I want to give you a little dose of reality that may feel heavy as you consider how you can improve your social media game. You might be surprised to hear me share this with you, but once you finally reach a certain level of comfort in using this new tool, you will never fully get a handle on it. You will feel like there is no way you can keep up with all of the moving parts. That's okay. Just embrace the insanity, knowing there is power in doing what you're doing with social media. The landscape of social media is organic. As it evolves, we must evolve as leaders.

We keep ourselves fresh by assuming the attitude of a student when it comes to using social media to grow our ministries. You will feel discouraged. You may even believe it's impossible to keep up. That's okay, too. You will never figure it all out. You will never master it completely. We don't use social media because we will perfect it; we use it for the good it can do for the kingdom. That alone is worth the effort. You will, however, make great strides in introducing an entire population of people to the gospel. That alone is worth the effort.

Legendary NFL coach, Vince Lombardi said it like this: "Perfection is not attainable, but if we chase perfection, we can catch excellence."[1] I long to see a nation of ministry leaders who rise up and learn to reach out with excellence. Are you up for the challenge?

Why Facebook?

According to current trends, Americans spend an average of two hours each day on social media. That means that people in your church are spending more time on social media in one day than they spend at your church in a whole week! By creating a presence on social media, you can be faithfully present in the lives of your church (as well as community) members each day, making it a powerful tool. Why would you want to miss that opportunity?

I will spend the majority of my time in this book referring to Facebook practices and tips. Facebook continues to dominate in the social media space, reaching one billion people every day. You may find yourself overwhelmed with all of the social media platform options. Don't be. Choose one platform and master it. Use it well. Grow from there.

THE QUESTION **THAT COULD CHANGE EVERYTHING**

Most churches or ministries have realized they are missing the mark when it comes to the effective use of social media. In an attempt to suddenly be culturally relevant, a well-intentioned person will create a page and begin posting to it with very little thought given to detail. As a result, we do what we often do in church: we do things the way we've always done them. That's dangerous territory for the church. Our message is too great and the hope people need to know about is too important to haphazardly approach our entry into the world of social media. To do so causes more harm than good.

Many churches use their Facebook pages as if they were a flashing billboard. Our culture doesn't respond to such advertising, especially on social media. That's why it is usually unsuccessful. Social media platforms were not designed to serve as constant commercials or scrolling billboards. Instead, social media is most effective when it invites others into a shared space where healthy, lively conversation takes place. The more diverse the audience, the more robust the conversation, thus creating a successful social media ministry.

Stop using social media as a primary means of communication with people who are already in your church, posting content that is "insider" focused, and using social media as a form of your church bulletin. Instead, use it with the Great Commission in mind. When we are willing to diversify our approach and invite others into our space, we'll begin to see real success in our social media platforms.

In order to use social media to its full capacity, we must ask ourselves this one question: Who am I trying to reach?

Why did you decide your church needed a social media presence? If you are hoping to use social media to reach out to others, why would you post prayer requests from your church members? Why would you continue to post "help wanted" ministry ads? Why would you post about all of your upcoming events? Why would you post your cleverly designed acronyms or Christianese? If you determine social media is a means of reaching out, rather than reaching in (toward members who are already present), then you've got to post content that is helpful to that demographic of people. Here are three problems with posting information that targets your congregation:

1. **You are missing opportunities.** You're missing the chance to reach people who have no idea about their need for Christ.
2. **You appear insider focused.** Think of it like this: would you like to walk into a party where everyone knows everyone else but you don't know a soul? Everyone in the room knows where to find anything they need but you don't have a clue. No one wants to enter a situation like that, much less a church. Understandably, your congregation is going to know one another and hopefully, enjoy being in relationship with one another. But as the "front door" of your ministry, your social media content should not demonstrate this "insider focused" view. I realize your church may have some killer acronyms (I say this in jest. You do realize your clever acronym is only clever to you, right?!), but stop using them if your objective is to reach out. Church lingo is horribly insider focused and further isolates church from unchurched folk.
3. **You feed the consumer mentality.** Often, those who attend church do so with a "have it your way" mentality. Using social media to reach out subtly teaches church members that their church exists for others, too. Church leadership is very aware of the consumeristic problem within our churches. When we design everything from our worship music set to our social media content, there is little reason to wonder why.

It's been said that social media is not a megaphone, but rather, a telephone. If you've determined to use social media as a means of reaching out, everything you do should be designed to initiate a conversation. You are inviting others into a conversation designed to either encourage, inspire, or familiarize them with your ministry.

So, who are you trying to reach? No, really, answer that question right now. If your target audience is people who are not yet members of your church, you will post content to share hope, create engagement, and facilitate community among people in a digital space.

If your answer is people in your church, then ask yourself why. Why would you not want to use a tool to reach countless people you would not otherwise have access to? Are you looking beyond the care of your own flock? The Great Commission reminds us of our mandate to reach lost people. Let's allow that to motivate us.

The truth is, your Facebook page is going to reach people outside your church. The real question is, do you want to harness its power for good or harm?

Start Here

- Answer this question: Who are you trying to reach?
- Define how social media is a ministry for your church. Share this with church leaders.
- Visit the Facebook pages of churches in your area. Scroll through their feed and see if you can determine for whom their social media ministry exists. Is it insider focused or unchurched driven content?

SIX WAYS
SOCIAL MEDIA SETS
THE TABLE

D o you remember the first time you felt invisible? For me, it was in the lunchroom of Fairfield Jr. Sr. High School. I was a brand new seventh grader in a new (to me) school building. It was overwhelming. The biggest question I had was, where was I going to sit? Picture this scene with a slew of insecure middle school girls who were all hoping to belly up to the table next to the popular kids. As my peers jockeyed for position at the lunchroom table, I felt like I didn't belong. It seemed like my presence in that lunchroom had no bearing upon anyone else.

Have you ever felt that way? I know a lot of people who live this way. They are on the outside looking into a world of church folk who seem to have their acts together. They're curious and intrigued but see the table as full. They can't possibly envision a spot at the table for themselves. Church, let's pull up as many chairs as we can. Let's look outside of our circles and invite others in. Let's make room for conversation—even if it might get messy.

Truthfully, most unchurched people feel undervalued by the church. Let's welcome unchurched people to our tables by inviting them into discussions that matter. In so doing, we are saying, "Your opinion matters here." Conversations open doors. When doors are open, tables are shared. There is plenty of room at Christ's table.

As pastors, we should always look for ways to invite others to our table. By harnessing the power of social media, we create that space. The effective use of social media in your ministry will set your table in the following six ways:

1. **Convey positive information**. People desperately want to hear positive truths. As people climb into bed at night, they're grabbing their phones. As they open their Facebook apps, they're being bombarded with negativity that often feels like a noose. What if our ministries were able to turn that around by becoming beacons of hope? Using your church's social media to convey hope helps to lift the weightiness of life. It's all about giving. Is there another church in town doing something amazing? How about highlighting it? Share news about a teacher who has gone the extra mile in your local school. Showcase the story of a volunteer in your community who continues to make a difference.

2. **Disciple people.** It is possible for social media to be both evangelistic as well as purposeful in developing disciples. You could do this by hosting private Bible studies (set up as private groups that people join) for people who are already in your church body. Why not use any means possible to help people grow deeper in their faith? Provide links to new Bible studies or webinars that may interest people. Providing tools to help Jesus followers grow in their faith is worthy of our attention.
3. **Foster a sense of community.** Ideally, a physical community would develop, but why not intentionally foster online community when the opportunity arises? People are longing for places to belong. During a recent livestream event I participated in, a gentleman who had recently lost custody of his children and was battling addiction entered the chat area. He started asking questions like, "If God is a loving God, why do bad things happen to innocent people?" Instead of shutting him down because he was asking questions, we allowed him to express doubt and concern. We wanted him to know this online space was a safe space for him to ask things he normally hadn't asked in a traditional church setting. During the service, we reached out to this man and invited him to coffee to further the discussion. The goal of this online ministry was not to tell him about an upcoming men's event or even to indicate that we would share Jesus with him if he came to our physical church building the next Sunday but, rather,

to invite him into this online community where he could feel safe and know we would steward his questions well.

4. **Embrace social interaction.** Interact with others. Social media was never intended to be a one-way street. Many people have the impression that churches are full of people who are close-minded. When we enter into social online spaces, we can create an atmosphere that invites interaction and discussion. If our churches (and online church spaces) aren't capable of handling doubt and questions, perhaps it's time to revisit what we do altogether.

5. **Become community-aware:** What do the people in your community care about? What needs could you help to meet through social media? Short of taking out billboards that say things like "First Baptist loves Chicago," you won't have the opportunity to express community love and support the way social media will allow. Post/like/comment as your church/ministry on community-based pages to show your concern.

6. **Make your ministry more approachable.** Reaching unchurched people only occurs when we peel back the layers and let them see who we are: real people with really messy lives. So much of what we need to do on social media involves tearing down previously erected walls—walls that have separated "us" from "them" for far too long.

Start Here

- Using Facebook, find any/all city or community pages. Usually, you can do this by clicking the search box and typing your city name. Facebook will generate lists of pages. Select as many as you'd like and simply "like" those pages. This will give you insight into your community in a way you don't normally receive. Their posts will now show up in your news feed. Establish a presence. Make comments, share their posts over on your ministry page, or simply like what they're posting.
- Using Facebook, find one of your local school pages. Repeat the steps listed above.
- Find something positive happening in the life of your community or even a local business, and celebrate that on your page.

GETTING **STARTED**
DIVING IN • FIRST STEPS

WHAT, HOW, AND **HOW OFTEN TO POST**

You've answered the question, "For whom does this ministry exist," right? You now have a laser-like focus that will determine what you post. Congrats. Many churches never even make it this far. You're on the right track. You are well on your way to social media ninja status—a worthy title few in ministry world ever achieve because they're busy designing cute acronyms and feeding consumer-Christians who are already warming their pews.

Before you become too self-confident, let's consider the next step. What will you post? This step often slows people down. Determining a steady stream of inspiration-worthy content creates fear in the minds of the strongest of leaders. The very idea that this is an ongoing, day after day, week after week struggle is enough to cause even the strongest of leaders to retreat. This paralysis results in churches who post inconsistently and without any thought given to offering value-based content.

Let's start by stopping. Stop using social media to blast information designed to inform and, instead, replace it with information designed to equip and inspire. Less information; more conversation. Spending time weekly or monthly laying out all of the content you will post will solidify your position as the social media ninja you know you want to be.

In his book, *Jab, Jab, Jab, Right Hook: How to Tell Your Story in a Noisy Social World,*[1] Gary Vaynerchuk teaches that in order to earn the right to present what you offer (in our case, ministry on a deeper level—the gospel message), you must repeatedly contribute in a positive sense. My teenagers are great at asking for things. I am more inclined to listen to their pleas when they've presented themselves as contributing members of the family. When your ministry actively shows up and is seen as a contributing member of your community, people will begin to take notice. You will have earned the right to speak into their lives.

Many churches assume that posting their upcoming events is equivalent to having an effective social media presence. This is not the case. Think about it like this: Do you love being in a relationship with someone who constantly asks for something? "Can you come to this?" "Will you help me with that?" "Can I tell you about this upcoming event?" Our world is full of people who assume the church is always asking for something. We further contribute to this mindset when we approach social media this way.

What if we began, instead, to approach social media from the standpoint of giving back? What if the desired outcome became building others up? Encouraging our communities? Discipling church folk? In doing just that, I believe we would be invited into the lives of community members like never before.

Let's get the party started. Grab your calendar and determine your content for seven days' worth of posts. A good rule of thumb is to produce content that is:

- 30% Informational
- 30% Conversational
- 30% Inspirational
- 10% promotional

So, if you were to design posts for each day of the week, they may contain content that looks something like this: two informational posts, two conversational posts, two inspirational posts, and one promotional post.

Informational Content Ideas:
- Did you know . . . ?

Conversational Content Ideas:
- Would you rather . . . ?
- What keeps you from . . . ?

Inspirational Content Ideas:
- Scripture
- Small nuggets and quotes from Sunday's message.

Promotional Content Ideas:
- Join us for family movie night!

Let's Get Practical

Learn to build your content and posts around various themes and you will save a lot of time. For example, August is typically back to school month for most areas. Sit down in July and develop a content schedule designed to support the back to school theme.

One post could list the number of pencils Americans purchase during the month of August. People love silly information that lightens the heaviness of their news feed. Another post could include pictures of your local school buildings with the caption, "Who will commit to praying for Anderson High School this week as teachers head back to school?" You could post pictures of local teachers who may be a part of your church. Interview them and ask them to share how they got into teaching. On the first day of school, ask people to share pictures on your church's page or to share them on their page and then tag your church. You could post scripture verses about the value of learning and wisdom. See how easy that was? Just think of the fun you could have (for more theme ideas, see the Appendix).

It happens to all of us in positions that exercise creativity in some sense. We sit down to crank out a bunch of information and we stare at the screen, unsure of how to proceed. When you schedule a day each week or month to line up all of your social media, you will free up your creative mind and will ensure this doesn't happen to you. Learn to curate content.

The best way to curate content is to open a file in something like Evernote. Evernote is a great tool that enables you to access important information from your various devices.

Evernote is the perfect spot for you to take notes, gather ideas, and archive notable information as you come across it. As you gather ideas, you simply start new notes. By doing so, you always know where to look when it comes time to find that great idea you came across a couple of weeks ago. Think of Evernote as a sticky note that you can access from practically anywhere. As you see something that you want to remember, post a link to that particular article/blog post or resource you want to share within Evernote and access it at any time. Titling notes within Evernote as something like "Facebook discussion starters" or "helpful links for our Facebook page" will help you curate information so that you won't ever run short of useful content.

Starting an Evernote file for favorite sites is helpful. Take some time and post links to your favorite websites. Then, when you sit down to do your scheduling for the week or month, visit these sites to grab links or generate graphics to get you going. Curating information as you see it will make a world of difference. This will enable you to get out from behind the proverbial eight ball.

How Often Should You Post?

Consistency is key here. Posting to Facebook no less than once per day and no more than three times per day is a great rule of thumb. For platforms that move quicker, like Twitter, you may consider posting more frequently. Be *very careful* to not over post. No one wants to feel like they're being bombarded with your announcements all of the time. But when you post content that adds value to the lives of people, you won't have to worry. By following the 30/30/30/10 principle mentioned above, you earn the right to share with your community.

Start Here

- Using your calendar of choice, design seven days' worth of posts for your ministry. Specifically, list what each post will say for the week. Allow about one hour until you get the hang of this. After some time, you will be able to do this in a much shorter amount of time.
- Schedule it. Mark your calendar for one week from right now that reminds you to repeat this process next week.
- Begin a "swipe file" to curate content. Open an Evernote (or similar) notebook and start to list websites where you find valuable content.

TEN TIPS TO DEVELOP KILLER POSTS THAT INCREASE ENGAGEMENT

5

Imagine inviting friends to a party, but only one friend shows up, and when they do, you leave the room, leaving that person to wonder where everyone is. There is no food, there is no music. Just a party invitation and crickets. When we post things that are not designed to create engagement, we miss a huge opportunity. Being intentional about posts to create engagement will drive conversation and true community.

1. **Know your audience.** When you know your audience, you will tailor design each post. "If you aim at nothing, you're sure to hit it every time," says legendary leadership guru Zig Ziglar.[1] Don't make the

mistake of wasting your message on the wrong group. Know your audience's needs, hurts, and pain points. When you have a real handle on this, you'll have a much easier time designing content.
2. **Tell a story.** Stories resonate with people. Tell stories about your church and the people within. Share "my life before Jesus and after" stories. Teach your congregation to share its stories using social media.
3. **Keep it simple.** T.M.I. is valid when it comes to social media posts. Squeezing too many details into posts only serves to confuse people. Rather than really reading to decipher what it is you're trying to say, they will keep scrolling instead.
4. **Keep it short.** The shorter, the better. People are scrolling at rapid rates as they scan their news feeds. They won't stop to read long posts. People like bite-sized nuggets of information.
5. **Ask open-ended questions.** People want to know their opinions are valued. Asking open-ended questions invites people into the familiar "living space" of your church and allows them to get cozy for a moment as they share a bit about who they are.
6. **Use emojis.** Statistics show that posts that use emojis are read more often. Don't overuse them. If you do, it will become obvious and you'll just be annoying.
7. **Write in second person.** Inviting people into conversation means including them. When you write in second person, you are opening your online space so people know there is room for them as well.

8. **Use pictures to tell stories.** Real pictures of real people who are a part of your church will generate interest. Just make sure your congregation knows you might use their images on social media and give them the opportunity to opt out.
9. **Make it personal.** Share from your heart, being transparent and authentic as you post. People will catch on quickly if what you do is too institutional.
10. **High touch over high tech.** Leonard Sweet & Frank Viola advised, "The strength of the church is not the strength of its institutions but the authenticity of its witness."[2] Always err on the side of being authentic. It's normal to not feel qualified to offer ministry via social media. You don't need to have all of the answers to show up and be a witness in the lives of unchurched people. Showing up is done by simply liking and commenting on posts or comments made by people. Just being present in an online space helps foster a sense of community.

Start Here
- Develop two posts this week using second person language.
- Develop one post that tells a story. Maybe a story about how someone found your church, or a story about someone who felt hopeless until they met Jesus and how their life is different today.
- Develop one post that asks an open-ended question. Keep in mind that it doesn't have to be super serious. People like talking about pizza toppings and ice cream.

BECOMING **MULTILINGUAL**
(OR LEARNING TO SPEAK FACEBOOK)

Nothing can be more overwhelming than the idea of learning how to master a new skill. Nothing, that is, except mastering said new skill while throwing in a bunch of language and terminology that is foreign. Adding new lingo to the mix takes it to another level. By learning what just a few key words mean, you will be navigating Facebook business-page world in no time at all. Here are some terms you should familiarize yourself with:

- **Post likes**. By clicking the "like" button below a post, people are sending a virtual high five. It's a way to say, "Hey, I enjoy this content" without posting a comment. Each time someone "likes" one of your posts, Facebook takes notice and will begin to share your content in the news feeds of others who like your page.

- **Page likes**. Page likes signify the number of people who are wanting to receive updates from your page. Consider them to be fans of your ministry or church. Page likes are intentional and require a Facebook user to choose to follow a particular page. People may unlike your page at any time just as easily. The more page likes you have, the more your page will be seen as credible. The number one way to gain page likes, thus increasing your exposure, is by posting great content. When you add value to the lives of people by posting content that is relevant, they will share your content and you will gain followers as a result.
- **Share.** If someone clicks the "share" button on one of your posts, your original post will show up in the news feed of that person's friends. This is a win-win for you because it's reaching people you normally don't have access to. Creating shareable content should always be your goal.
- **News feed.** This is the stream of stories you see on Facebook. When posting as your church or ministry business page, your posts show up in the news feed of those who like your page.
- **Algorithms.** Let's say your page has 200 likes. Of those 200, Facebook decides who sees your posts. Your content will be seen by a very small percentage of the 200 people who like your page. That's why it's important to produce content people want. Once your posts begin to receive some traction (people are liking,

commenting, or sharing), Facebook's algorithms will pick up on that, believing it to be important and then begin showing it to more people. People spend their lives trying to uncover the mystery of Facebook algorithms. No need to get that kind of crazy. Just keep up as much as possible with what seems to be trending regarding your posts.

- **Analytics**. Facebook provides you with an outstanding analytics tool to help you know what's working and what's not. The "insight" tool is available to business page owners with minimal followers and can be found toward the top of your business page (not your personal page).
- **"Tagging" a photo**. Clicking on a picture you're posting enables you to select and name people who are in that picture. Why does this matter? Because, once again, this information shows up in news feeds of people who aren't already a fan of your ministry page. When I tag Abby Martin in a photo on our page, Abby Martin's friends see that she was tagged in a photo by First Presbyterian Church. That might lead them to click on it to see more about Abby Martin's awesome youth group or church.

Start Here

- Define page likes. How many does your page currently have?
- Identify how many likes a recent post had on your page.
- Find the "insights" tool at the top of your page.

DESIGN **HACKS**

"I don't have an artistic bone in my body."

If you've ever uttered those words, I can relate. If that is what holds you back as you think about beefing up your ministry's social media presence, worry no more. In the day and age in which we live and minister, there have never been more tools at our fingertips designed to help the artistically-challenged produce designs that look like you actually know what you're doing. By learning to use a few tools and apps, you'll become a design pro in no time.

Do not assume you can simply Google images and use those. These are copyrighted images and you could wind up in trouble by using them.

Here are some apps and web-based design-helps that will make the process so much easier.

Apps
- Word Swag
- Adobe Spark Post
- Artists
- Canva
- Kanvas Lab
- PicMonkey
- Typeorama

Web
- Canva (www.canva.com) is a free dynamic tool you can use for social media, flyers, book covers, and a lot more.
- Unsplash.com has free, high-quality images to use in a variety of projects.
- Lightstock (www.lightstock.com) provides one free Christian image per week and one free video clip per month when you give them your email address.
- Church Butler (www.butler.church) allows you to purchase (for as little as $20/month) ready-made social media content for your church's platforms.
- Sunday Social (www.sundaysocial.tv) provides a $9/month subscription for ready-made JPGs you can add your own church logo to and post as your own.

Start Here
- **Start a note on your computer.** Set up a Pinterest board for inspiration. On days when you feel short

on inspiration, use the content you posted within the note to help warm up your brain. Pin scripture or other Christian resources on this board.

- Load the above-mentioned apps onto your phone and start playing around with them.
- Begin searching for someone who could generate inspirational graphics in batches. This person could do thirty images at a time, for example. This will be more than you will actually need (remember not all of the content that you post will be inspirational). Once you have a point-person, start to build a team around him or her to lighten your load.

ELEVEN OF THE MOST COMMON MINISTRY PAGE MISTAKES

Sometimes the path to success is made easier by defining obstacles we may face. Designing an effective social media ministry is much the same. By listing some of the mistakes churches often make, I hope to help make your path a little smoother. By just being proactive and intentional, you can avoid many of these most-often made mistakes.

1. **Blasting announcements.** The purpose of social media is not to serve as a billboard. Just think about how annoying commercials are when you're trying to watch TV. Stop all of the advertisements! We all have that one friend who blows up our news feed

with their MLM products. You don't want your ministry to be seen as "that friend."

2. **Insider info/lingo.** People feel like they're not a part of your community when you post content that excludes them—posts such as inside jokes, prayer requests, names of events that make no sense to anyone except church attenders, etc. All of them just add to a feeling of disconnect.
3. **Inconsistent, outdated posts.** Posting once every few weeks does more harm to your cause than help. Post things that are relevant. And do so consistently.
4. **Post text only.** The human eye is drawn to images. Use lots of them! Your posts will show up more in the news feed of others more often when an image is attached. Don't just post scripture. Use one of the design tools mentioned in Chapter 7 to create something people will actually be drawn to.
5. **Not engaging in conversation.** Social media is just that: *social*. Be present and interact. Once you've posted, it's important to "like" people's replies. It's also important to reply or comment as the discussion continues. Don't just start a conversation and "leave the room." This can be accomplished by checking in a couple of times throughout the day. Don't feel that you must constantly be scrolling social media news feeds. A couple times a day is all it takes.
6. **Post only serious content.** One of the greatest criticisms of church folk is that we are simply not relatable. Post funny things and down to earth content that dispels that myth.

7. **Using "Christian-ese."** Overused, Christian niceties are not the way to reach into your community. We further isolate ourselves when we use Christianese as a normal part of our conversation. Stay away from trite Christian jargon that further isolates people from feeling like they could become part of our communities.
8. **Posting content that no one wants to share.** (Insider focused or just downright boring.) Most people will share things that present them in a positive light. Make sure your content is "share worthy."
9. **Being argumentative.** It's not the goal of social media to win arguments regarding politics or social justice issues. Our goal is to invite people into a conversation. Many ministries dive into heated debates or discussions that have no business in online spaces. These sorts of conversations are better experienced in coffee shops. Chances are pretty good you will not win someone over to your way of thinking on a social media platform. When stewarding our online space, we must get rid of our desire to prove someone wrong or our attempts to educate them. It's not our place.
10. **Not using social media.** It's where people hang out. Why wouldn't you want to be there as well?
11. **Grow your page by inviting "insiders."** Many ministry leaders aren't sure how to grow their following on social media, as a result, they resort to the "invite friends to like this page" option. *Don't do it.* Work to ensure the number of likes you have on your page are

legitimate. Aunt Irene from Idaho doesn't really count. If the purpose of your page is to establish a presence among your community members, do that. Your family already thinks you're awesome. You don't need their "like."

Church leaders do not need to add "one more thing" to their growing to-do list. Just the thought of it can be overwhelming. The good news is that limited time and resources are easily overcome by using the right strategy. Don't make these social media mistakes.

Use social media as a means to reach the multitudes by going where people are, offering great content that encourages and inspires, and showing your community support.

Start Here

- Google "Christianese." I'm serious. Do it. As you read through these lists and posts, think about the language you use. Is it "insider Christianese?" If so, your posts will not reach their intended audience.
- Resist the urge to post any church announcements this week. Zero.
- Visit another church Facebook page using the eyes of a visitor or unchurched person. Notice the language and pictures that church uses. What do those posts convey?

PAGES OR GROUPS? YES.

Should we use a Facebook "Page" or "Groups"? The short answer to this question is yes. Pages and Groups are both valuable tools. If you're just getting started, I'd suggest beginning with Pages. Pages are easily searched within Facebook, making it easier for someone who may be searching for your church to find you without too much effort. And they are better for ministry outreach (which, I assume if you're still reading this book, is your goal).

Six Tips to Develop a Quality Page
- Design your header using Canva (www.canva.com). This will ensure that the graphic is designed proportionally and will look its best.

- Try to stay away from stock images when designing a header. Using tools like Canva allows you to create personalized images with minimal effort.
- Use a clean image that doesn't have too much going on in it.
- Use the "About" option to write as much as you can about your church or ministry. Remember, you are trying to break down walls. Increasing the comfort level of those who might be exploring your church or ministry is made easier when you allow people to get a sense of "who" you are and what a typical day in your ministry is like.
- Stay away from "church" sounding words in your description. Talk about Jesus and faith freely, but try to stay away from words such as "fellowship" or words like "foyer" or "sanctuary"—all of which further isolate us from the community we are hoping to reach.
- Take advantage of the "Email Signup" feature on the left-hand side of your page. Even though social media is powerful, research still shows that email communication remains the number one way to effectively communicate with people. As long as Facebook continues to use algorithms to limit the number of people who see your content, you will not have full control. Emailing someone allows you to have direct access to him or her without having go through the Facebook middleman in hopes of reaching your intended audience. A couple of the most popular platforms are MailChimp and ConstantContact. Setting up the Email Signup feature is pretty simple. Most churches use an

email platform that allows them to send group email messages. Those platforms are easily linked with your ministry Facebook page. A simple YouTube search for (the name of your email platform provider) along with Facebook integration will provide you with step by step tutorials to get you started. Don't miss this step!

When to Use a Group Instead of a Page
Groups are great for communicating "insider" information. Maybe I've crushed your hopes and dreams about using Facebook as a means whereby you can communicate freely with your congregation. In an attempt to redeem myself in your eyes, I'd offer this: there is a place for social media when it comes to just being able to get information out to people.

Groups are great for the individual ministries within your church. I'd encourage you to not have more than one page to represent your church. This waters down your attempt to get your message out. The women's ministry, men's ministry, knitting club, kid's ministry, etc., are often better served by using Groups.

Experts on social media marketing still seem to agree there should be one main church page with everything being filtered through it. I tend to agree. Work diligently to get each ministry leader to understand who you are targeting with your Facebook content. Otherwise, people will be constantly asking you to blast information that doesn't fit with what you're trying to accomplish.

Groups can be set up using a variety of privacy settings. Here is a brief description of the differences:

- **Closed Facebook Groups.** When a group is closed, only people who have been invited to the group can see posts and content. And nobody can post to the group unless he or she is part of the group. Any Facebook user could search for the group, enabling the user to see such a group exists, but they would be unable to see anything within the group if they are not a member.
- **Secret Facebook Groups.** When a Facebook group is secret, it can only be seen by those in the group. Even if a Facebook user searches for the group, it will not be listed.
- **Public Facebook Groups.** Any Facebook user can see the members of a public group as well as what has been posted. However, he or she will not be able to post within the group without being a member.

Some Advantages to Groups
- **Groups can be great places for "insider" information.** If you want to provide a place to offer prayer requests or more announcements to those who already attend your church, by all means, set up a Group. You can set the privacy settings to meet your needs, as described in the previous section.
- **Groups are great opportunities for discipleship.** Use Groups for things like online short-term Bible Study. For example, set up a group called "First Steps." Give an explanation on your main page talking about the First Steps group. Design it to be a closed group that will serve as a six-week Bible Study that explores

the basic tenets of faith. Weekly, post a two- or three-minute video introducing the topic regarding faith formation that you are highlighting. Then post comments and questions once per week supporting that topic. You'll find that people who aren't able to attend or who have never considered attending a Bible Study may enjoy the opportunity to sort of ease into matters of faith. Groups are wonderful tools for discipleship. I encourage you to use Groups designed for people who aren't currently searching but who are already part of your church or ministry.

Think of Groups as a microphone and Pages as a megaphone. With your Page, you want to broadcast to a larger, further extending audience. With your Group, you simply need to get the word out to those already in the room. This all goes back to your intent and who you're hoping to reach.

SUSTAINING
MOMENTUM

CUTTING DOWN ON CONTENT CHAOS
LEVERAGING TOOLS TO MASTER CONTENT MANAGEMENT

Let's face it, ministry involves a lot of unexpected, unplanned occurrences throughout the day. We cross off our to-do list items and we begin scribbling information for the next day before our heads hit the pillow each night. It never seems to end. The beautiful thing about living in the twenty-first century is, "There's an app for that." Learning how to schedule all of your posts will become a game changer for you. Trust me, business leaders are not sitting in front of their computer waiting to hit the "publish" button. Most social media leaders schedule their posts ahead of time to create more mind space for the matters that require their full attention in ministry.

By using media management tools, you can streamline your social media post scheduling and not have to worry about posting daily. Most of us don't have the time nor the emotional/mental capacity to be creative daily when it comes to posting. Using these tools makes all of the difference. Scheduling all posts days or weeks ahead of time allows you to focus on the unexpected surprises that occur in the life of a pastor.

Your calendar is your friend: using a calendar, mark off each day you've scheduled your posts. This will help ensure that you post consistently. Ultimately, you could do this monthly in a couple of hours.

If your primary social media platform is a Facebook page, go into Facebook as if you were going to write a new post. A blue arrow will show up on the bottom right-hand side of the post. From there, you can schedule posts on whatever day and time you like. (There is much discussion about whether or not Facebook's algorithms are affected by things like natively posting from Facebook versus using a managing tool. No one knows for sure, but most people say posting to Facebook through Facebook's scheduler will produce better results, causing your post to be seen by more people.)

Optional Tools to Manage Social Media Posting:
- HootSuite (hootsuite.com)
- Buffer (www.buffer.com)
- TweetDeck (www.tweetdeck.com)
- Grum (Instagram scheduler) (www.grum.co)
- Sprout Social (sproutsocial.com)

Learning to use one of these tools (or simply using the scheduling tool within Facebook) is the ultimate brain dump experience. Once you have everything loaded into your social media accounts using one of these schedulers, you will not need to give it another thought (other than commenting as people interact). Spending a few hours each month (I suggest the last week of the month so you can prepare for and schedule the next month's content), will free you to engage in your other ministry duties. Finally, sit back and enjoy the freedom that comes from knowing your to-do list just got shorter for the next month.

Start Here

- ○ Choose one of these management options and set up an account today. Watch a brief YouTube tutorial on how to schedule posts.
- ○ Find a calendar and mark each day that you've scheduled. Be specific and write the actual post content on your calendar.
- ○ Schedule one week's worth of posts by writing each one on the calendar.

THREE TRICKS
TO GAIN MOMENTUM

"**O**h, pick me. Pick me!"

Remember those days on the playground when you waved your hand wildly in the air? I feel like that a lot of days when it comes to using social media effectively. So much of what I do is trying to influence the algorithms of Facebook as well as my fans or followers. I want to teach you how to gain momentum when you need it most—right before a big event or sermon series. If the objective is to get the word out, learning how to master this is critical.

You will always have a need to get the word out about various events on your church calendar—Easter is on the horizon, small groups are starting back up after summer break, or you have a parenting seminar that you're offering to your community. Here are three tips to help you gain the momentum you need: obtain reviews, create events, and utilize the power of your ministry leadership.

1. **Reviews.** They are a big deal. Are you an Amazon user? Whenever I am preparing to purchase an item for the first time, I will not do so without having read at least a few reviews. People do the same thing when they consider visiting your church. They want to know what other people think. Work hard to build up your reviews on your Facebook page over the next week.

   When people review your church or ministry, the fact that they did so will show up in the news feed of their friends who may not already be fans of your page. Imagine an unchurched person seeing content such as the following review of Anderson First Church of the Nazarene in his or her news feed: "First Church is the best. It is the most caring, welcoming, friendly, loving, gracious church I have ever had the pleasure of being a member of. Thanks to all who make it the best church anywhere."

   Reviews matter. Don't be afraid to ask for them. Having at least a handful of reviews on your page establishes some credibility if someone were to be looking at your page. If you're just getting started with your Facebook page, ask a handful of current church members to write a review. This will "prime the pump" so to speak. When visitors show up, they are more likely to write their own review if they see some reviews already on your page.

2. **Events.** Facebook's event tool is a great way to inform people about upcoming events your church or ministry is hosting. While we don't want to go overboard when it comes to promoting our own content, highlighting special events is a great way to gain momentum on social media.

When creating an event for your page, you will have the option of "inviting" people to the event. The people who are invited will also be given the opportunity to invite their friends. And as they accept your invitation, it will show up in the news feed of some of their friends. Can you see how this is pure advertising magic? Creating an event on Facebook and explaining the details is pretty simple. Using design tools like Canva, create a placeholder image for your event so that it looks sharp in people's news feeds.

Your church can even dip its toe into the waters of paid ads on Facebook to generate even more interest in events.

Four Event Tips
- **Think outside the box.** Events don't have to be over-the-top productions. They can be anything from your Easter service to parenting seminars. Avoid the temptation to create an event for every single ministry offering in your church. This will hinder your efforts when you attempt to really make a big push for a special event.
- **Tag people in event photos.** Tagging will do two things. First, it will generate curiosity in what

your ministry has going. Second, it will push your content into the news feeds of more people. Post pictures from previous years' events as a way to generate excitement and interest.

- **Don't be shy about asking for comments.** When you have a large event coming up and you want to get the word out, don't be afraid of asking church members to comment on the event when you post it. When John says, "I wouldn't miss this event. It changed my life last year. I am a better dad and husband because I attended last year's 'Journey to the Summit.' I can't wait for this year's event!" it will speak more about the impact of an event than you could ever offer in a brief advertisement. Always mine great stories.
- **Ask for "shares."** Send private messages to church members saying something like, "We need your help. We are, once again, offering a free parenting seminar for members of the Indianapolis community. We are excited to foster new relationships and to nurture previous ones. Would you help us get the word out? You can help in one of the following ways: 1) Just hit the "share" button and maybe comment on how excited you are to be attending, 2) Hit the "share" button and tag some friends you think might benefit, or 3) Copy the event link and send a personal invitation via private message, text, or email to friends who might enjoy the event. We have an exciting message to share and hope you'll partner with us as we spread the word."

3. **The power of your ministry leadership.** In an attempt to tell a new story and reveal exactly who they are and why they do what they do, General Electric recently began looking for ways to invite the average American in to see what happens at G.E. Sam Olstein, the director of innovations for the company, explained the rationale behind this newest initiative by saying: "When you give people a peek behind the curtain, they fall in love with the company."[1] *Inviting the average community member to see what happens in your ministry and to understand your story moves people to want to learn more about who you are and why you do what you do.*

Want to give people a chance to fall in love with your church or ministry? Give them peeks behind the ministry curtain. People want to see your church staff and leadership in action. Posting video or pictures of them in action throughout the week will give you a bump in social media momentum. When your senior leadership speaks, people will pay attention. For people who are not yet familiar with your ministry, this is the equivalent of introducing them to one of your lifelong friends. This is yet another way to help people outside of your church feel welcome.

Six Ways to Leverage Leadership

1. When you have a big event coming up, text your leadership to let him or her know that you've just posted something about the event. Ask that person to hop on Facebook and comment from his or her personal

account about how exciting it is to be a part of this upcoming event. When people see that your leadership has commented, Facebook's algorithms will take it from there and push your content out to even more people. Asking staff members to comment or share events or topics of special interest will help you gain momentum quickly.

2. Post "happy birthday" announcements on your church's Facebook page for each of your pastors. Include a picture of each one. And ask people to share birthday greetings. (While this may appear to have the feel of "insider" information, others will take notice of the community banter, encouragement, and the love being shared).

3. Ask your pastor to share a thirty-second greeting during the week of Thanksgiving (and during other major holidays). A quick video that is shot with nothing more elaborate than the camera on your phone could potentially garner more views than anything you have posted in quite some time.

4. Have your pastor post a quick reflection on a passage of scripture and ask people to comment with any questions they may have.

5. Have church leaders give a quick behind-the-scenes tour of one of your ministry areas as people are preparing for worship services. People love "guided" tours by someone in leadership.

6. Have some fun. Take random pictures of various leaders' desks and ask people to guess which desk belongs to which pastor. Or post baby pictures of various leaders and have people guess which leader that person is.

Start Here

- Get three new reviews. When people understand how important this is, they're generally happy to help. Ask them to give you five stars if your ministry is worthy and to write a one or two sentence blurb about what makes your church so special.
- Create an event. Learn how to write a good description and include an event photo at the top. Good descriptions are brief and explain the "benefit" to the reader. Always include a graphic you design using a tool similar to one of the ones mentioned prior for your event.
- Ask a few key leaders to share a current post. Let them know when you've just published a post. When they hop on and share the post, it will help you gain momentum quickly.

USING VIDEO
IN POSTS

At this point, Facebook favors video (meaning it will show your videos to more people than any other content you may post). This may change tomorrow, so it would be wise for us to take advantage of knowing this right now. Short video clips grab the attention of even the most lackadaisical of scrollers.

Making short video clips is easier than you might think. Consider using one of the tools or apps listed below and create a small video clip. Try creating a short video just quoting Scripture. You don't have to make it too complicated.

Seven Ways to Use Video in Your Posts

1. Post a YouTube clip featuring a song that is part of this coming Sunday's worship set. People love to discover new music. And they love feeling like they've been given some "insider information" regarding the upcoming service. Give it to them!
2. Do a quick "behind the scenes" tour of the youth pastor's office. Have your children's pastor do a quick highlight of a new resource that would be of benefit to parents. Snippets from the church office or staff members are of high value. People want to see and know real people.
3. Share a short video of one of the staff pastors sharing a quick word of encouragement from Scripture.
4. Share a video of one of the pastors asking for prayer requests in the comments. Don't make this long and drawn out. Keep it short.
5. Conduct a Facebook live Q & A. Share from Scripture and have people comment with any questions or thoughts they may have. This is a great way to increase interaction among people who may not normally be inclined to do so.
6. Broadcast your service via Facebook Live (be sure your CCLI license includes streaming rights). Remember the saying "perfect always becomes the enemy of the good" when it comes to live streaming. Use whatever equipment you have. Start with a phone and tripod.
7. Communicate the story of your church often. Testimonies of others are excellent ways to share Jesus in online spaces.

Tools for Video

Apps:
- Adobe Spark Video
- iMovie
- Adobe Premiere Clip
- Ripl

Web:
- animoto.com

Live Streaming:

Learning to harness the power of video on Facebook can be a game changer for your ministry. Live video is currently one of the most powerful means of getting Facebook's algorithms to take notice. Many churches are afraid to go live for a myriad of reasons. Most of the church leaders who read this book will be leaders of smaller congregations. I want to assure you that it's OK to just start with what you have. Don't worry about producing movie-quality video. Stop comparing yourself and your ministry to others. Embrace who you are as a leader and your ministry context. Someone in your sphere of influence needs to know about your ministry. The possibilities of people who might join your worship service are infinite. Here are the reasons I hear most often for not live streaming:

1. **Many churches don't believe they have the proper equipment**. People don't care! Isn't that great news?! We somehow have it in our minds that in order to go live, we've got to have expensive, fancy equipment. This is simply not the case today.

In fact, there are many, for whom, the overly-produced appearance of a service is a turn-off. Bust out a phone and a tripod to get started. No shame in that game.

I realize that many of you will never have the opportunity to purchase high-end production equipment. Though there are many options out there when it comes to your ability to live stream and the equipment you can use, I'd encourage you to jump right in with what you have and take advantage of this untapped ministry opportunity.

2. **Many churches are afraid of what people might think of their service.** People are looking for authenticity. Pastor, I realize that leaders of megachurches are those who are in the limelight. They seem cutting edge—offering cool stage lighting and design. But someone in your community is looking for an authentic leader. One who communicates truth and who is willing to become vulnerable so that others might come to know the hope that can be found in Jesus. Do not let fear of what you believe you aren't able to offer hold you back in this area. You'll be surprised at how open to your church someone may become because of a live video feed.

3. **Some leaders are afraid people won't attend church in the physical church space.** Truthfully, this may happen from time to time. It will not become the norm. Don't let this fear hold you back from seizing the opportunity that live streaming offers. To me, this one seems silly. It's like refusing preventative dental treatment because I'm afraid I might get

a cavity. The potential still exists but I'd be crazy to make decisions regarding dental care around that possibility.

All three of these mindsets are based on fear. You, my friend, are not a fear-based leader. You see the opportunity to reach out in new ways. Pop your phone on a tripod, place it in landscape mode, and get started.

Tips to Get Started Live Streaming
- **Spend a couple of weeks announcing that you're going live.** People will become excited. Enjoy the synergy found in sharing an exciting, new step with your congregation.
- **Be aware of copyright issues.** Your church probably already has a CCLI license that enables you to play or perform music during your service. For a very small annual fee, you can also include live streaming of your services as part of your membership. This is worth the investment. Just be careful when using tools such as YouTube during your sermon illustrations. You are not covered to use these as part of your live stream.
- **Have someone available in the online chat space.** I can't stress this enough. One of the keys to using live streaming effectively is to create a shared social space. Social implies that there will be communication and dialogue that takes place. Don't just set up your live feed and disappear. The objective is to get people to interact. Here are some ways to do that:

- Offer a description such as "Worship at _____ 8/27/17." If you're in week two of a sermon series, you could post that as part of your description. If you know the direction of the message, you could even ask a question such as "Ever wonder what God meant when He said to love your enemies?"
- "Good morning. Welcome to worship at _____. We are so glad you could join us."
- Comment on the sermon series you're in the middle of.
- "Shout out to you joining us this morning on our live feed. Where are you watching from?"
- (During the prayer time of your service) "Prayer is an important part of who we are at _____ Church. We'd love to pray for your needs or concerns this week. Comment or message us and we will commit to doing just that."
- (During the offering) "Regular attenders of _____ often enjoy giving online. We invite you to do so by using this link: (post link)."
- Do not use insider lingo (including making the assumption that people know who is speaking, etc.). Assume that people attending online do not know the pastor, or do not know how quirky your youth pastor is and that everyone likes to poke fun at him or her. Introduce people who are part of the service. "We are celebrating the babies in our congregation this morning. Angie Masters is our nursery director. She has an amazing ministry to families with little ones. We are so grateful for her service."

- Upon the conclusion of the service, say something like, "We enjoyed having you join us today at _____ for worship. We trust you experienced a place where you know you belong. If we can be of help to you in any way in the days ahead, feel free to reach out. Until next week, (sign your name—more personal than your church's name)."
- Ask people to share your live feed. Here is how this will work; Your page will send an alert to everyone who follows your page, saying "Main Street Church of God is live." Once people see this, they will have the opportunity to share this live feed. Sharing the live feed becomes a great way for people to invite their friends to church.
- If a technical problem occurs during your live feed, just apologize and move on. Though it can be super frustrating, most people will understand. Make every attempt to stay on with the original stream, but if you have to begin a new one, be willing to do so.

Live streaming is less overwhelming than it may seem. There is so much potential in it. My question for you is, why would you *not* be willing to live stream?

In closing, I want to address an issue I hear about on occasion. So many of the pastors I talk with are quite unsure about "counting" people in online spaces. I would caution you to approach this with the utmost integrity. If you decide that you are offering an online church experience, learn what the numbers mean. "Views" may mean something different than you think. Spend time talking with others in online spaces and consult with denominational leadership. The important thing about considering online viewership is consistency. Do not assume that you can count all of the "views" of your service as "attendees."

Start Here

- Download one of the apps mentioned above. Create a thirty-second video clip to post this week.
- Designate a live stream person. Ask that person to find one other person who could shoot the service in his or her absence. These people will need to be given admin privileges on your page. Choose them wisely.
- Designate an online community moderator. Find a person who understands and embraces the objective of initiating conversation throughout the live stream of your service. Have that person begin to build a small team. The online moderators will also need to be given admin privileges on your page. Choose them wisely.

MEASURING
SUCCESS

Yeah, I realize we say we shouldn't care about numbers. The truth of the matter is, numbers matter. Generally speaking, numbers indicate health. Facebook is great at helping you with analytics. Why should this be important to you? Because knowing how many people are seeing your posts and engaging with them will help you grow your page, determine the content people are interested in, and help you spread your message even further.

From your ministry's Facebook page, select the option listed along the top called "Insights." Within Insights, you will be able to determine the number of "likes" your page has (or new likes received within a certain time period), the time of day most of your fans were active, and the number of times your content may have been shared. You can select each individual post and see how it compared to others. This becomes helpful because it allows you to see what sorts of content people were excited about and engaged with.

The Insights tool is one you will want to visit often. It will help you determine success as you post from month to month. You may be surprised when the posts you *just knew* were going to be hugely successful totally bomb.

You will also want to check in with your overall page likes from time to time. If your page's likes trend downward at any point, try to determine why. Was it the type of content you were posting? Were you posting too much? Was it maybe just them? Asking lots of questions while perusing Insights will help provide answers.

How to Deal with Haters

One of the things that prevents many ministries from becoming active on social media is the fear of having to deal with negative comments or the opinions of others. If we were to run every area of our ministry like this, we would be in great danger of not reaching anybody. The truth of the matter is that being in any sort of public space runs the risk of negative interactions. The online space is no different. You will face some sort of negativity at some point on social media. Here are some tips to help deal with that.

1. Expect it. It will happen.
2. Don't take it personally.
3. Don't react too quickly. Knee-jerk reactions are not advised. Take your time, cool off if you need to (remember, this isn't personal) and, in a timely manner, offer a reply.

4. Address negative comments in a public space. Don't shy away from negative comments. (If someone is undermining the character of another person, that's an exception. In that case, it is acceptable to delete the comment and kindly state the ethics of page participation.) Acknowledge each comment.

5. Remember, the way you react or reply will say a lot about who you are as a church community.

6. Don't be quick to delete comments that are negative. Big corporations don't block and delete every negative comment written about their company. Why should we?

7. Draft a few replies ahead of time so you won't have to think in the moment.

Some of the best marketing happens in the midst of controversy. Be present in the online space and don't shy away from it. Respond with kindness and authenticity. People will notice.

Start Here
- Get into Insights. Play around for a bit and familiarize yourself with the options found therein.
- Compare two recent posts. Can you tell what made one more successful than the other?
- Determine what time of day most of your followers are using Facebook.

BUILDING A SOCIAL MEDIA **MINISTRY DREAM TEAM**

14

The best ministry leaders are the ones who realize they don't have to do everything themselves. A wise pastor is willing to delegate communicating via social media to capable volunteers. Selecting people to be the "face and voice" of your church may seem frightening but it doesn't have to be.

One key piece of information when building a team is this: do *not* give access to your ministry's social media accounts to too many people. The more people you involve, the more likely that people will post more often about "pet projects." If the youth pastor is an admin on your church's social media platforms, he or she will often only see his or her particular piece of the ministry puzzle rather than the bigger picture. Find a social media manager. Work with that person and turn him or her loose. Don't micromanage. Social media management is often a subjective arena. Pastors, don't weigh in with your opinions. Give your social media manager freedom to do his/her job without feeling the need to offer your opinion on everything.

Tips for Choosing Social Media Managers
1. **Select people with outstanding character.**
2. **Train them to know and own the "why" behind your page.** It's critical that anyone with access to your social media accounts understands the big picture. For whom are they posting? Spend lots of time ensuring this is understood.
3. **Give them the tools they need.** Teach them to use the apps mentioned throughout this book. Give them a list of Facebook groups and podcasts that they can refer to and share content from. Resource them and turn them loose.
4. **Do not think you own this ministry.** Ministry never belongs to us. Your role is to develop leaders as the shepherd of your church and then send them out.

Start Here
- Find one person you can develop as your social media manager.
- Train that person, asking him or her to always keep this question in mind: "For whom does our social media ministry exist?"
- Resource that person with the ideas found at the end of this book, online help, podcasts, and apps.

CLOSING

Perhaps Erik Qualman said it best: "We don't have a choice whether we do social media, the question is how well we do it." Church leader, you're leading today, in your particular context, in this particular year "for such a time as this" (Esther 4:14). It's time to take the reins, gather your courage, and realize the potential of the land that lies before you. You'll find so much excitement as you learn to use new tools to do the work of the Master.

May the words of the apostle Paul encourage you as you launch this new ministry. "Be wise in the way you act toward outsiders; make the most of every opportunity. Let your conversation be always full of grace, seasoned with salt, so that you may know how to answer everyone" (Colossians 4:5-6).

Making the most of every opportunity,

Jill

READY-MADE
CONTENT IDEAS

PART 4

CAMPAIGNS

15

Note to reader: *All quotes mentioned below can be found through a basic Internet search. Popular sites include www.goodreads.com and www.brainyquote.com.*

The use of social media campaigns designed around sermon series or spiritual concepts is a useful way to steward your social media content. If your theme for the next two weeks is "The Love of God" for example, you could post one question, two quotes, two scriptures, and resources on how people can better embrace the concept of God's love. This would give you one post per day for a week's worth of time, all designed around one theme that will enhance the spiritual lives of all who are a part of your page.

Using social media in ways such as this drives both evangelism as well as discipleship within your local church. I don't share these ideas in an attempt to dictate your sermon series, but rather, to stimulate your thought process when it comes to how you might tie your current preaching series into what you offer on social media. Here are fifteen ready-made campaigns for you. I didn't get very specific in the articles/ideas segments because the very best articles or ideas are often timely pieces. I've included generic sessions for each campaign.

Campaign Topics
- Serving Others (pg. 92)
- Answering God's Call (pg. 94)
- Holy Living (pg. 96)
- Your Prayer Life (pg. 98)
- Anxiety/Worry (pg. 99)
- God's Love (pg. 101)
- The Church (pg. 102)
- Forgiveness (pg. 105)
- The Holy Spirit (pg. 106)
- Temptation (pg. 108)
- Parenting (pg. 110)
- Marriage (pg. 111)
- Heartache (pg. 113)
- Friendship (pg. 115)
- Hope (pg. 116)

Serving Others

Questions: (Post one of these questions per week)
- Sometimes allowing others to serve us is tough. When do you find it most difficult to allow others to serve you?
- Serving others often brings about unexpected joys in our own lives. Has there ever been a time when you were unexpectedly blessed because you served someone else?

Quotes: (Post one of these every couple of days)
- "The purpose of life is not to be happy. It is to be useful, to be honorable, to be compassionate, to have it make some difference that you have lived and lived well." (Ralph Waldo Emerson)
- "No one has ever become poor by giving." (Anne Frank)
- "There is no exercise better for the heart than reaching down and lifting people up." (John Holmes)
- "No one is useless in this world who lightens the burdens of another." (Charles Dickens)
- "You have not lived today until you have done something for someone who can never repay you." (John Bunyan)
- "If you're not making someone else's life better, then you're wasting your time. Your life will become better by making other lives better." (Will Smith)

Scripture: (Using one of the design tools mentioned previously, create a graphic using one of these scripture references. Post one every couple of days.)
- "God is not unjust; he will not forget your work and the love you have shown him as you have helped his people and continue to help them." (Hebrews 6:10)
- "You, my brothers and sisters, were called to be free. But do not use your freedom to indulge the flesh; rather, serve one another humbly in love." (Galatians 5:13)
- "Therefore, I urge you, brothers and sisters, in view of God's mercy, to offer your bodies as a living sacrifice, holy and pleasing to God—this is your true and proper worship." (Romans 12:1)

- "The greatest among you will be your servant." (Matthew 23:11)
- "For even the Son of Man did not come to be served, but to serve, and to give his life as a ransom for many." (Mark 10:45)

Resources:

Google applicable, relevant articles or videos about someone whose service made a difference in the life of someone else. Providing links to spiritual gifts inventories may prove helpful as well. People may not be serving because they don't understand how they're wired. Using social media to resource Christians is a wonderful opportunity. Share links to these online inventories to equip people.

Answering God's Call

Questions: (Post one of these questions per week)
- What stops most people when it comes to responding to God's call on their lives?
- Many times we struggle to know what the will of God is. How do you answer the question, "What is God's will for your life?"

Quotes: (Post one of these every couple of days)
- "There are no 'if's' in God's world. And no places that are safer than other places. The center of His will is our only safety—let us pray that we may always know it!" (Corrie ten Boom)
- "The will of God is not something you add to your life. It's a course you choose. You either line yourself up

with the Son of God . . . or you capitulate to the principle which governs the rest of the world." (Elisabeth Elliot)
- "For each one of us, there is only one thing necessary: to fulfill our own destiny, according to God's will, to be what God wants us to be." (Thomas Merton)
- "When God throws something your way, catch it!" (Chriscinthia Blount)
- "I will follow God's plan." (Jill Waltz)

Scripture: (Using one of the design tools mentioned previously, create a graphic using one of these scripture references. Post one every couple of days.)
- "In all your ways submit to him, and he will make your paths straight" (Proverbs 3:6)
- "Many are the plans in a person's heart, but it is the Lord's purpose that prevails." (Proverbs 19:21)
- "And my God will meet all your needs according to the riches of his glory in Christ Jesus." (Philippians 4:19)
- "For I know the plans I have for you," declares the Lord, "plans to prosper you and not to harm you, plans to give you hope and a future." (Jeremiah 29:11)
- "And we know that in all things God works for the good of those who love him, who have been called according to his purpose." (Romans 8:28)

Resources:

Pastors and staff, host a Facebook Live Q & A session on the will of God. Ask people to leave comments or questions on your page (or in a private message) about discerning the will of God. Tell people to tune in to your page on Thursday evening at 8:00 p.m. where someone will spend ten minutes answering some of these questions.

Holy Living

Questions: (Post one of these questions per week)
- We often hear about Scripture calling us to live differently than the rest of the world. What does it mean to "live differently?"
- What does the word "holy" mean to you?

Quotes: (Post one of these every couple of days)
- "Holiness does not consist in doing extraordinary things. It consists in accepting, with a smile, what Jesus sends us. It consists in accepting and following the will of God." (Mother Teresa)
- "Holiness, as taught in the Scriptures, is not based upon knowledge on our part. Rather, it is based upon the resurrected Christ in-dwelling us and changing us into His likeness." (A.W. Tozer)
- "It's not the things I don't understand about the Bible that bother me; it's the things I understand with perfect clarity and don't comply with that keep me up at night." (Bill Hybels)
- "When a brave man takes a stand, the spines of others are often stiffened." (Billy Graham)
- "God does not want you to become a God; he wants you to become godly—taking on his values, attitudes, and character." (Rick Warren)

Scripture: (Using one of the design tools mentioned previously, create a graphic using one of these scripture references. Post one every couple of days.)

- "But just as he who called you is holy, so be holy in all you do." (1 Peter 1:15)
- "But you are a chosen people, a royal priesthood, a holy nation, God's special possession, that you may declare the praises of him who called you out of darkness into his wonderful light." (1 Peter 2:9)
- "May God himself, the God of peace, sanctify you through and through. May your whole spirit, soul and body be kept blameless at the coming of our Lord Jesus Christ." (1 Thessalonians 5:23)
- "Create in me a pure heart, O God, and renew a steadfast spirit within me." (Psalm 51:10)
- "Therefore, I urge you, brothers and sisters, in view of God's mercy, to offer your bodies as a living sacrifice, holy and pleasing to God—this is your true and proper worship." (Romans 12:1)

Resources:

Google relevant articles about people who are currently making tough choices—choices that demonstrate they are living above the "just good enough" mentality that many Christians have. Posting links to books on holiness will also be valuable.

Your Prayer Life

Questions: (Post one of these per week)

- Are there times when prayer is harder for you than others? What do you do when that happens?
- What do you think it means to pray in Jesus' name?

Quotes: (Post one of these every couple of days)

- "Prayer should be the key of the day and the lock of the night." (George Herbert)
- "To have God speak to the heart is a majestic experience, an experience that people may miss if they monopolize the conversation and never pause to hear God's responses." (Charles Stanley)
- "The greatest tragedy in life is not unanswered prayer but unoffered prayer." (F.B. Meyer)
- "Nowhere is it more important to be in a conversational relationship with God than in our prayer life." (Dallas Willard)
- "Prayer is not asking. Prayer is putting oneself in the hands of God, at His disposition, and listening to His voice in the depth of our hearts." (Mother Teresa)

Scripture: (Using one of the design tools mentioned previously, create a graphic using one of these scripture references. Post one every couple of days.)

- "This, then, is how you should pray: 'Our Father in heaven, hallowed be your name, your kingdom come, your will be done, on earth as it is in heaven. Give us today our daily bread. And forgive us our debts, as we also have forgiven our debtors. And lead us not

into temptation but deliver us from the evil one.'" (Matthew 6:9-13)
- "The eyes of the LORD are on the righteous, and his ears are attentive to their cry." (Psalm 34:15)
- "This is the confidence we have in approaching God: that if we ask anything according to his will, he hears us." (1 John 5:14)
- "He went away a second time and prayed, 'My Father, if it is not possible for this cup to be taken away unless I drink it, may your will be done.'" (Matthew 26:42)
- "The prayer of a righteous person is powerful and effective." (James 5:16)

Resources:

Google relevant stories of the power of prayer. Post links to books on prayer and to blog posts talking about the importance of or how-to. Ask how your church or ministry can best pray for people that week.

Anxiety/Worry

Questions: (Post one of these per week)
- When was the last time you remember not worrying about anything?
- What particular part of your life causes you the most anxiety?

Quotes: (Post one of these every couple of days)
- "Worrying is carrying tomorrow's load with today's strength—carrying two days at once. It is moving into tomorrow ahead of time. Worrying doesn't empty

tomorrow of its sorrow, it empties today of its strength." (Corrie ten Boom)
- "The more you pray, the less you'll panic. The more you worship, the less you worry. You'll feel more patient and less pressured." (Rick Warren)
- "Our anxiety does not empty tomorrow of its sorrows, but only empties today of its strengths." (Charles Spurgeon)
- "Our anxiety does not come from thinking about the future, but from wanting to control it." (Kahlil Gibran)
- "Fear not the future. God is already there." (Billy Graham)

Scripture: (Using one of the design tools mentioned previously, create a graphic using one of these scripture references. Post one every couple of days.)
- "Therefore I tell you, do not worry about your life, what you will eat or drink; or about your body, what you will wear. Is not life more than food, and the body more than clothes?" (Matthew 6:25)
- "Who of you by worrying can add a single hour to your life?" (Luke 12:25)
- "Peace I leave with you; my peace I give you. I do not give to you as the world gives. Do not let your hearts be troubled and do not be afraid." (John 14:27)
- "Cast your cares on the Lord and he will sustain you." (Psalm 55:22)
- "Cast all your anxiety on him because he cares for you." (1 Peter 5:7)

Resources:

Google relevant articles on worry and anxiety. Direct people to books written from a Christian perspective on how to deal with worry.

God's Love

Questions: (Post one of these per week)
- When was the last time you truly felt loved by God?
- What do you find the hardest to believe about the way God loves you?

Quotes: (Post one of these every couple of days)
- "Though we are incomplete, God loves us completely. Though we are imperfect, He loves us perfectly. Though we may feel lost and without compass, God's love encompasses us completely . . . He loves every one of us, even those who are flawed, rejected, awkward, sorrowful, or broken." (Dieter F. Uchtdorf)
- "We should be astonished at the goodness of God, stunned that He should bother to call us by name, our mouths wide open at His love, bewildered that at this very moment we are standing on holy ground." (Brennan Manning)
- "No matter what storm you face, you need to know that God loves you. He has not abandoned you." (Franklin Graham)
- "Though our feelings come and go, God's love for us does not." (C.S. Lewis)

Scripture: (Using one of the design tools mentioned previously, create a graphic using one of these scripture references. Post one every couple of days.)

- "But God demonstrates his own love for us in this: While we were still sinners, Christ died for us." (Romans 5:8)
- "But because of his great love for us, God, who is rich in mercy, made us alive with Christ even when we were dead in transgressions—it is by grace you have been saved." (Ephesians 2:4-5)
- "The LORD your God is with you, the Mighty Warrior who saves. He will take great delight in you; in his love he will no longer rebuke you, but will rejoice over you with singing." (Zephaniah 3:17)
- "See what great love the Father has lavished on us, that we should be called children of God! And that is what we are! The reason the world does not know us is that it did not know him." (1 John 3:1)
- "Give thanks to the God of heaven. His love endures forever." (Psalm 136:26)

Resources:

Post links to articles on love. You could use the stories of the way a parent sacrificially loves his or her child to demonstrate God's love.

The Church

Questions: (Post one of these per week)

- What do you see as the biggest challenge "the church" faces today?

- What importance has the church played in your personal faith development?

Quotes: (Post one of these every couple of days)
- "Church attendance is as vital to a disciple as a transfusion of rich, healthy blood to a sick man." (Dwight L. Moody)
- "The perfect church service, would be one we were almost unaware of. Our attention would have been on God." (C.S. Lewis)
- "Wherever we see the Word of God purely preached and heard, there a church of God exists, even if it swarms with many faults." (John Calvin)
- "One hundred religious persons knit into a unity by careful organization do not constitute a church any more than eleven dead men make a football team. The first requisite is life, always." (A.W. Tozer)
- "Nothing on earth has greater potential to change lives and carry out His kingdom work in your community, than your local church. There's nothing like the local church when it's working right. Its beauty is indescribable. Its power is breathtaking. Its potential is unlimited. No other organization on earth is like the church. Nothing even comes close." (Bill Hybels)

Scripture: (Using one of the design tools mentioned previously, create a graphic using one of these scripture references. Post one every couple of days.)
- "And let us consider how we may spur one another on toward love and good deeds, not giving up meeting

together, as some are in the habit of doing, but encouraging one another—and all the more as you see the Day approaching." (Hebrews 10:24-25)
- "And God placed all things under his feet and appointed him to be head over everything for the church." (Ephesians 1:22)
- "... built on the foundation of the apostles and prophets, with Christ Jesus himself as the chief cornerstone. In him the whole building is joined together and rises to become a holy temple in the Lord. And in him you too are being built together to become a dwelling in which God lives by his Spirit." (Ephesians 2:20-22)
- "Let the message of Christ dwell among you richly as you teach and admonish one another with all wisdom through psalms, hymns, and songs from the Spirit, singing to God with gratitude in your hearts." (Colossians 3:16)
- "... so in Christ we, though many, form one body, and each member belongs to all the others." (Romans 12:5)

Resources:

This campaign lends itself to asking really great questions and creating dialogue around what the church should be. Who we were designed to be. Perhaps some articles on how we've become consumeristic in our approach would be in order. Google some relevant articles and post links. Get the discussion going. One really great advantage to this is that unchurched people can see that your community is a great place to ask questions or to even express doubt.

Forgiveness

Questions: (Post one of these per week)
- When have you experienced an act of forgiveness that seemed truly unbelievable to you?
- Why do you think forgiveness is so difficult for most people?

Quotes: (Post one of these every couple of days)
- "Always forgive your enemies; nothing annoys them so much." (Oscar Wilde)
- "Forgiveness is the name of love practiced among people who love poorly. The hard truth is that all people love poorly. We need to forgive and be forgiven every day, every hour increasingly. That is the great work of love among the fellowship of the weak that is the human family." (Henri J.M. Nouwen)
- "To be a Christian means to forgive the inexcusable because God has forgiven the inexcusable in you." (C.S. Lewis)
- "Forgiveness is an act of the will, and the will can function regardless of the temperature of the heart." (Corrie ten Boom)
- "Forgiveness is not an occasional act, it is a constant attitude." (Martin Luther King, Jr.)

Scripture: (Using one of the design tools mentioned previously, create a graphic using one of these scripture references. Post one every couple of days.)

- "Be kind and compassionate to one another, forgiving each other, just as in Christ God forgave you." (Ephesians 4:32)
- "But if you do not forgive others their sins, your Father will not forgive your sins." (Matthew 6:15)
- "If we confess our sins, he is faithful and just and will forgive us our sins and purify us from all unrighteousness." (1 John 1:9)
- "Do not judge, and you will not be judged. Do not condemn, and you will not be condemned. Forgive, and you will be forgiven." (Luke 6:37)
- "And forgive us our debts, as we also have forgiven our debtors." (Matthew 6:12)

Resources:

Google relevant articles on forgiveness. You should even be able to find a lot of really good, short videos highlighting acts of forgiveness. If you know someone in your church who was forgiven greatly or who has a story to share on how they learned what it meant to forgive, this would be a great time to share that story.

The Holy Spirit

Questions: (Post one of these per week)
- What do you think is the role of the Holy Spirit in the life of a Christian?
- What do you think people find the most confusing to understand about the Holy Spirit?

Quotes: (Post one of these every couple of days)
- "It is the Holy Spirit's job to convict, God's job to judge, and my job to love." (Billy Graham)
- "The wizard [of Oz] says look inside yourself and find self. God says look inside yourself and find [the Holy Spirit]. The first will get you to Kansas. The latter will get you to heaven. Take your pick." (Max Lucado)
- "Those in whom the Spirit comes to live are God's new Temple. They are, individually and corporately, places where heaven and earth meet." (N.T. Wright)
- "The Holy Spirit will always point people to the finished work of Jesus." (John Paul Warren)
- "The Spirit inspired the Word and therefore He goes where the Word goes. The more of God's Word you know and love, the more of God's Spirit you will experience." (John Piper)

Scripture: (Using one of the design tools mentioned previously, create a graphic using one of these scripture references. Post one every couple of days.)
- "But you will receive power when the Holy Spirit comes on you; and you will be my witnesses in Jerusalem, and in all Judea and Samaria, and to the ends of the earth." (Acts 1:8)
- "Those who live according to the flesh have their minds set on what the flesh desires; but those who live in accordance with the Spirit have their minds set on what the Spirit desires." (Romans 8:5)
- "But as for me, I am filled with power, with the Spirit of the Lord, and with justice and might." (Micah 3:8)

- "But the Advocate, the Holy Spirit, whom the Father will send in my name, will teach you all things and will remind you of everything I have said to you." (John 14:26)
- "And hope does not put us to shame, because God's love has been poured out into our hearts through the Holy Spirit, who has been given to us." (Romans 5:5)

Resources:

Google some solid teaching articles that explain the nature of the Holy Spirit or point to the functions of the Holy Spirit. People really do want to understand things like the Holy Spirit and other matters of faith that seem shrouded in mystery. Use this social media campaign to disciple as well as evangelize. Keep in mind that all of us learn differently—use some video clips as well as written articles. Using sermon clips for those who are auditory learners is also a great means of teaching.

Temptation

Questions: (Post one of these per week)
- How do you think Christians can learn to recognize temptation?
- How do you personally resist temptation?

Quotes: (Post one of these every couple of days)
- "There is a charm about the forbidden that makes it unspeakably desirable." (Mark Twain)
- "... the devil doesn't come dressed in a red cape and pointy horns. He comes as everything you've ever wished for ..." (Tucker Max)

- "The road to success is dotted with many tempting parking spaces." (Will Rogers)
- "Opportunity may knock only once, but temptation leans on the doorbell." (Unknown)
- "Temptation always starts in your mind. Not in circumstances." (Rick Warren)

Scripture: (Using one of the design tools mentioned previously, create a graphic using one of these scripture references. Post one every couple of days.)
- "Watch and pray so that you will not fall into temptation. The spirit is willing, but the flesh is weak." (Matthew 26:41)
- "No temptation has overtaken you except what is common to mankind. And God is faithful; he will not let you be tempted beyond what you can bear. But when you are tempted, he will also provide a way out so that you can endure it." (1 Corinthians 10:13)
- "And lead us not into temptation, but deliver us from the evil one." (Matthew 6:13)
- "Put on the full armor of God, so that you can take your stand against the devil's schemes." (Ephesians 6:11)
- "Blessed is the one who perseveres under trial because, having stood the test, that person will receive the crown of life that the Lord has promised to those who love him." (James 1:12)

Resources:

Google relevant articles on steps to overcome temptation. You could keep things fairly light with this topic and, perhaps, offer a post along the lines of "top food temptations" and ask people to share what their toughest temptation to battle in the food department might be.

Parenting

Questions: (Post one of these per week)
- What is the toughest parenting lesson you've learned?
- What makes someone a good parent?

Quotes: (Post one of these every couple of days)
- "Until kids find something worth dying for, they don't have anything worth living for." (Tim Kimmel)
- "Show your children God's love by loving them and others as Christ loves you. Be quick to forgive, don't hold a grudge, look for what's best, and speak gently into areas of their lives that need growth." (Genny Monchamp)
- "God doesn't want us to rescue our children. He's the Rescuer." (Elizabeth Musser)
- "The future belongs to people with children, not with things. Things rust and break." (Archbishop Charles Chaput)
- "As a mother, my job is to take care of the possible and trust God with the impossible." (Ruth Bell Graham)

Scripture: (Using one of the design tools mentioned previously, create a graphic using one of these scripture references. Post one every couple of days.)
- ". . . and how from infancy you have known the Holy Scriptures, which are able to make you wise for salvation through faith in Christ Jesus." (2 Timothy 3:15)

- "Start children off on the way they should go, and even when they are old they will not turn from it." (Proverbs 22:6)
- ". . . because the Lord disciplines those he loves, as a father the son he delights in." (Proverbs 3:12)
- "These commandments that I give you today are to be on your hearts. Impress them on your children. Talk about them when you sit at home and when you walk along the road, when you lie down and when you get up. Tie them as symbols on your hands and bind them on your foreheads." (Deuteronomy 6:6-8)
- "Children are a heritage from the Lord, offspring a reward from him." (Psalm 127:3)

Resources:

You should be able to find a plethora of ideas about parenting when Googling this one. Parenting help is one of the greatest needs of the community in which you minister. Post links to practical books and other parenting resources.

Marriage

Questions: (Post one of these per week)
- What is the biggest lesson you've learned through your marriage?
- What do you think is the biggest misconception regarding marriage?

Quotes: (Post one of these every couple of days)
- "A good marriage is the union of two good forgivers." (Ruth Bell Graham)

- "When I have learned to love God better than my earthly dearest, I shall love my earthly dearest better than I do now." (C.S. Lewis)
- "Christian marriage is marked by discipline and self-denial. Christianity does not therefore depreciate marriage, it sanctifies it." (Dietrich Bonhoeffer)
- "A good marriage isn't something you find; it's something you make." (Gary L. Thomas)
- "In Christian marriage, love is not an option. It is a duty." (R.C. Sproul)

Scripture: (Using one of the design tools mentioned previously, create a graphic using one of these scripture references. Post one every couple of days.)

- "Be completely humble and gentle; be patient, bearing with one another in love. Make every effort to keep the unity of the Spirit through the bond of peace." (Ephesians 4:2-3)
- "And over all these virtues put on love, which binds them all together in perfect unity." (Colossians 3:14)
- "Husbands, love your wives, just as Christ loved the church and gave himself up for her." (Ephesians 5:25)
- "Therefore what God has joined together, let no one separate." (Mark 10:9)
- "Love is patient, love is kind. It does not envy, it does not boast, it is not proud. It does not dishonor others, it is not self-seeking, it is not easily angered, it keeps no record of wrongs. Love does not delight in evil but rejoices with the truth. It always protects, always trusts, always hopes, always perseveres. Love never fails." (1 Corinthians 13:4-8)

Resources:

Consider asking people if they would like someone to pray for their marriage. Give them the option of sending you their request via private messenger. Google relevant, practical, and helpful articles and practical, helpful articles and offer them as a way of reaching out.

Heartache

Questions: (Post one of these per week)
- What is the most practical way someone has encouraged you as you walked through a season of heartache?
- What one promise of God has sustained you through periods of heartache?

Quotes: (Post one of these every couple of days)
- "The greatest good suffering can do for me is to increase my capacity for God." (Joni Eareckson Tada)
- "I trust in you, Lord, but keep helping me in my moments of distrust and doubt." (Henri Nouwen)
- "I learned to trust that, through God's grace, something beautiful and new would emerge even in the face of my weakness, tears, pain and hopelessness. I too would live again." (Bethel Crockett)
- "What we have once enjoyed and deeply loved we can never lose, for all that we love deeply becomes a part of us." (Helen Keller)
- "For me, laughter is how we take a much-needed break from the heartache, such that when we turn to face it again, it has by some miracle grown smaller in size and intensity, yet not disappeared altogether." (Liz Curtis Higgs)

Scripture: (Using one of the design tools mentioned previously, create a graphic using one of these scripture references. Post one every couple of days.)

- "But he said to me, 'My grace is sufficient for you, for my power is made perfect in weakness.' Therefore I will boast all the more gladly about my weaknesses, so that Christ's power may rest on me." (2 Corinthians 12:9)
- "The LORD is a refuge for the oppressed, a stronghold in times of trouble. Those who know your name trust in you, for you, LORD, have never forsaken those who seek you." (Psalm 9:9-10)
- "Though I walk in the midst of trouble, you preserve my life. You stretch out your hand against the anger of my foes; with your right hand you save me. The LORD will vindicate me; your love, LORD, endures forever—do not abandon the works of your hands." (Psalm 138:7-8)
- "Why, my soul, are you downcast? Why so disturbed within me? Put your hope in God, for I will yet praise him, my Savior and my God." (Psalm 42:5)
- "The LORD is my strength and my shield; my heart trusts in him, and he helps me. My heart leaps for joy, and with my song I praise him. The LORD is the strength of his people, a fortress of salvation for his anointed one." (Psalm 28:7-8)

Resources:

For this particular campaign, it would be powerful to offer a Facebook Live event in which you simply offer encouragement. Maybe share one or two scriptures about God's help in times of trouble and offer to pray for those who are experiencing heartache. Resources and books are also wonderful tools for people who are walking the road of heartache. Share links to helpful resources addressing this topic.

Friendship

Questions: (Post one of these per week)
- What was the name of your first friend?
- What character traits do you think are most important in a friend?

Quotes: (Post one of these every couple of days)
- "Friendship . . . is born at the moment when one man says to another 'What! You too? I thought that no one but myself . . .'" (C.S. Lewis)
- "I would rather walk with a friend in the dark, than alone in the light." (Helen Keller)
- "'Why did you do all this for me?' he asked. 'I don't deserve it. I've never done anything for you.' 'You have been my friend,' replied Charlotte. 'That in itself is a tremendous thing.'" (E.B. White, *Charlotte's Web*)
- "It is more fun to talk with someone who doesn't use long, difficult words but rather short, easy words like 'What about lunch?'" (A.A. Milne)
- "Sitting silently beside a friend who is hurting may be the best gift we can give." (Unknown)

Scripture: (Using one of the design tools mentioned previously, create a graphic using one of these scripture references. Post one every couple of days.)

- "My command is this: Love each other as I have loved you. Greater love has no one than this: to lay down one's life for one's friends." (John 15:12-13)
- "Walk with the wise and become wise, for a companion of fools suffers harm." (Proverbs 13:20)
- "Do to others as you would have them do to you." (Luke 6:31)
- "Be devoted to one another in love. Honor one another above yourselves." (Romans 12:10)
- "As iron sharpens iron, so one person sharpens another." (Proverbs 27:17)

Resources:

This topic lends itself to lots of articles or even some questions you could post that would spark conversation. Post a verse, such as Proverbs 27:17, then ask people to tag a friend who made them a better person. Google should lead you to some relevant articles on this topic. One word of caution: be careful to not make this topic too touchy-feely. You could possibly polarize men and women when it comes to engagement on the topic of friendship. Women may be all over it and men may keep their distance.

Hope

Questions: (Post one of these per week)
- What gives you hope?
- Have you ever experienced a time when you felt hopeless? How did you turn that around?

Quotes: (Post one of these every couple of days)
- "Hope is the thing with feathers that perches in the soul and sings the tune without the words and never stops at all." (Emily Dickinson)
- "Only in the darkness can you see the stars." (Martin Luther King, Jr.)
- "Hope begins in the dark, the stubborn hope that if you just show up and try to do the right thing, the dawn will come. You wait and watch and work: you don't give up." (Anne Lamott)
- "If it were not for hope, the heart would break." (Thomas Fuller)
- "Hope is being able to see that there is light despite all of the darkness." (Desmond Tutu)

Scripture: (Using one of the design tools mentioned previously, create a graphic using one of these scripture references. Post one every couple of days.)
- "Many are saying of me, 'God will not deliver him.' But you, Lord, are a shield around me, my glory, the One who lifts my head high. I call out to the Lord, and he answers me from his holy mountain. I lie down and sleep; I wake again, because the Lord sustains me. I will not fear though tens of thousands assail me on every side." (Psalm 3:2-6)
- "Praise be to the God and Father of our Lord Jesus Christ! In his great mercy he has given us new birth into a living hope through the resurrection of Jesus Christ from the dead, and into an inheritance that can never perish, spoil or fade. This inheritance is kept in heaven for you." (1 Peter 1:3-4)

- "... the LORD delights in those who fear him, who put their hope in his unfailing love." (Psalm 147:11)
- "And hope does not put us to shame, because God's love has been poured out into our hearts through the Holy Spirit, who has been given to us." (Romans 5:5)
- "... but those who hope in the LORD will renew their strength. They will soar on wings like eagles; they will run and not grow weary, they will walk and not be faint." (Isaiah 40:31)

Resources:

This campaign lends itself to the telling of stories. Highlight the story of someone who once felt as if they'd lost all hope. Using Google, find relevant stories that you can highlight. Tools such as devotional books would also be great resources to link to.

101
CONVERSATION STARTERS

As I've mentioned several times throughout this book, social media should be designed to create conversations. The online space is a familiar, cozy place if we've done our jobs as social media ministers. One of the best ways to create this sort of online community is by asking open-ended questions. Here are 100 questions you can use to help generate a lot of discussion on your church's page. If you use these questions, I wouldn't use more than a couple of them a week. Too many of these light-hearted questions can almost become a distraction. Be sure you read all the way to tip #101. I've seen that particular idea generate more traction on a church's Facebook page than any other. Use these along with a graphic (using only a couple of words, if possible).

1. What friends are you the most thankful for? Tag them below and explain why they're so awesome.
2. If your week had a theme song, what would it be? (Post this on a Friday at lunchtime)
3. What exciting things do you have planned this weekend? (Post this on a Friday at lunchtime)
4. If you could learn to play one instrument what would it be?
5. Describe your weekend in three words. (Post this on Sunday evening or Monday morning)
6. Describe your weekend using a GIF in the comments below. (Post Sunday evening or Monday morning)
7. Describe your week using a song lyric. (Post on a Friday at lunchtime)
8. Name a trial you've gone through lately in which God has proven Himself faithful.
9. When was the last time you witnessed a random act of kindness? Share about the act below.
10. Where did you see God work this week?
11. Who could you be a blessing to today?
12. What is your favorite movie quote of all time?
13. Cake or pie?
14. Beach or mountains?
15. "'But what about you?' he asked. 'Who do you say I am?'" (Matthew 16:15)
16. Football or basketball?
17. What is your biggest question about faith?
18. What is on your must-read list that others should consider reading?

19. If you could have dinner with any influential person of faith (past or present), who would it be and why?
20. What is your favorite Bible reading tool?
21. What song best describes you?
22. What series are you currently binge watching?
23. Coffee or tea?
24. What one thing do you love most about _____ (the name of your church)?
25. When was the last time you were really nervous?
26. What has been your favorite movie of _____ (the current year)?
27. How can our ministry better resource you in your faith journey?
28. What is your favorite Christmas morning memory? (Post during the week of Christmas)
29. Are you a morning person or night owl?
30. What is your biggest struggle when it comes to your faith?
31. When it comes to food, do not ask me to share _____.
32. Toilet paper: over or under?
33. What did you study in college? If you had to do it all over again, would you study the same thing?
34. What is your favorite way to relax?
35. What is your go-to snack?
36. What is the hardest thing you've ever had to do?
37. Dogs or cats? Post a picture!
38. What is the last picture on your camera roll? Post it.
39. iPhone or Android?
40. Do you have a favorite day of the week? What is it?
41. What is your superpower?

42. When you need to de-stress, what do you do?
43. What is the most adventurous thing you've ever done?
44. Someone asks why you're a Christ follower. What do you say?
45. At what age did you decide to start living for Christ?
46. Who was your childhood hero?
47. What one thing are you doing today that will cause you to become more Christ-like tomorrow?
48. What song do you hope we sing tomorrow? (Post on a Saturday evening)
49. What one thing did you take away from the service or message today? (Post on a Sunday afternoon)
50. If you could pack your bags today and head anywhere, where would you go?
51. Who is joining us for worship in the morning? We hope YOU are! Comment below. (Post on a Saturday evening)
52. How do you think Jesus would tell people about Himself?
53. What is your Pandora Station of choice?
54. What three problems do you think most young people face today?
55. If you could ask Christ to change one problem, what would it be?
56. If you could do today over, what one thing would you do differently? (Post in the evening)
57. What is the strangest thing you've ever eaten?
58. If someone handed you $100 today and told you that you had to spend it today, what would you spend it on?
59. What was your first car? Extra points if you post a picture!

60. What is your least favorite household responsibility?
61. Which Bible character do you most identify with?
62. How do you define the word "Christian"?
63. What one question do you think God might ask you?
64. What one thing draws you closer to God than anything else?
65. What was the first scripture verse you memorized?
66. When do you feel furthest from God?
67. Favorite board game?
68. What was your most embarrassing moment?
69. What one character trait do you most admire in others?
70. How long have you been attending _____? (Church name)
71. What's one thing you could give that could help one person?
72. What would your last meal consist of?
73. What's your favorite love song? Why?
74. What is your most precious possession?
75. What would it take to become refreshed in your walk with Christ this week?
76. What is your favorite holiday? Why?
77. What is one thing about you most people don't know?
78. When did you first hear about Jesus?
79. What's the best advice you ever received?
80. When was the last time you saw prayer answered?
81. What word do you think God would use if He were to describe you?
82. Which biblical character do you wish you were more like?

83. Which passage of scripture do you have the most questions about? Any that leave you confused?
84. What things cause you the most frustration in your day-to-day life?
85. What is one food you refuse to eat?
86. What is your favorite breakfast cereal?
87. Who inspires you today? Tag that person in the comments below.
88. Would you rather live in the city or the country?
89. If you had a personal chef for the evening, what would you have him or her prepare?
90. What was your first job?
91. Do you have a trick to get the ketchup out of a new bottle?
92. Describe yourself with the name of a movie.
93. Coke or Pepsi?
94. What was the funniest prank you've ever been a part of?
95. You've only got two minutes in a grocery store and $10. What three items would you leave with?
96. Duct tape fixes everything. What have you used it to fix?
97. What is your biggest pet peeve?
98. Which is correct? Sock, sock, shoe, shoe? Or sock, shoe, sock, shoe?
99. What is the best compliment you've ever received?
100. If you could be any age for a week, what age would that be and why?
101. How can we best pray for you this week? Comment below and we assure you that someone will be praying. You can also share your request via Messenger or by emailing us at _____.

FUN
HOLIDAYS/EVENTS

Taking advantage of the things other people are talking about is a great way to gain momentum. People love posting things about "National This and That Day." Take advantage. Using holidays like the ones listed below, you're sure to generate some great discussion and increase engagement on your page. Here are some fun holidays along with some post ideas. You will find them practical and useful.

National Pizza Day (February 9th):
- What is your all-time favorite pizza joint?
- What are your "must have" toppings?
- What do you consider to be the strangest pizza topping?
- My favorite people to eat pizza with are _____.

Super Bowl Sunday (Typically the last Sunday in January or the first Sunday in February):
- Who are you pulling for in the big game?
- More importantly, what will you be snacking on?
- I love watching the game with _____. Tag the buddies you'll be watching with.

April Fools' Day (April 1):
- Fess up. When were you "gotten" by an April Fools' Day prank?

National Sibling(s) Day (April 10):
- Tag your brother or sister in the comments below. Tell them how they have enhanced your life.

National Donut Day (First Friday of June):
- What is your favorite donut shop?
- Cake or yeast?
- Favorite donut topping?

National Ice Cream Day (Third Sunday of July):
- What is your all-time favorite ice cream flavor?
- Do you have a favorite ice cream shop?
- Cone or cup?

World Emoji Day (July 17):
- We all love them! Post your most often used emoji.

National Grandparent's Day (Sunday after Labor Day):
- Did you have a favorite grandparent growing up? What made him or her so special?

National Coffee Day (September 29th):
- My favorite coffee shop is _____.
- My favorite coffee drink is _____.
- My favorite thing to do while drinking coffee is _____.
- Did you love coffee the first time you tried it or was it an acquired taste?
- I like a little coffee with my cream and sugar. Vote yes by hitting "like."
- My favorite person to enjoy a cup of coffee with is _____.

Black Friday (the day after Thanksgiving):
- We know you're out there today. Post a picture from your Black Friday escapades.
- What time did you start shopping?

National Teacher Day (First Tuesday in May):
- We are grateful for the teachers who have invested in our lives over the years. Tag a teacher who made an impact on your life.

Mother's/Father's Day:
- In what way does your mom/dad most resemble Jesus?
- In what way are you most like your mom/dad?
- What is the best advice your mom/dad ever gave you?
- What is the most special thing about your mom/dad?

Thanksgiving:
- Share your favorite Thanksgiving memory below.
- Share a picture of your Thanksgiving table.
- Share your favorite Thanksgiving recipe.
- Considering all of the names we use when we describe God's character, for which are you most thankful?
- Do you have an unusual Thanksgiving tradition? Share it below.
- What is your all-time favorite Thanksgiving food?
- Which Bible verse are you most thankful for?

Christmas:
- Share a picture of one of your childhood Christmases.
- Share a picture of your favorite Christmas cookie.
- What is your favorite Christmas song?
- What unusual Christmas tradition do you have?
- What is the most memorable Christmas gift you've ever received?
- What is your favorite Christmas movie?
- Who is your favorite character in the Christmas story?
- Which moment in the Christmas story is your favorite?

DAYS OF THE
WEEK THEMES

18

Using repeating fun themes based on the days of the week is a good way to keep discussion going on your ministry Facebook page. Once you start getting creative, you'll find that the ideas just keep coming.

#MotivatorMonday
- What one thing are you motivated to get done this week?
- What is your favorite, go-to motivational quote of all time?
- In what area are you lacking motivation today?

#MusicMonday
- If you were to describe your hope for this upcoming week, what song would it be?

- What song gets stuck in your head most often?
- What style of music is your least favorite?
- Describe your life in one music title.

#TruthfulTuesday:
- How many times per day do you log into Facebook?
- Did you ever eat glue when you were in school?
- What is currently in the trunk of your car?
- What is on your current playlist?
- What song do you currently have stuck in your head?
- Do you sing along with the songs at the grocery store?
- What is the #1 thing on your to-do list today?
- Did you exceed the speed limit this week? Vote yes by hitting the "like" button.

#WednesdayWisdom
- What one bit of wisdom would you share with your 5th-grade self?
- What is the best advice you ever received?
- What advice would you give to a graduating senior?

#WednesdaysWord
- What one scripture means the most to you right now?
- What one scripture did someone share with you in the past that changed your outlook on a particular situation?
- What was the first scripture you memorized?

#ThankfulThursday
- What one modern-day tool are you most grateful for?
- What season are you most thankful for?
- What one person are you most thankful for today?

#FlashbackFriday
- Share a picture from your first day of school.
- What was your first job?
- What did you want to be when you grew up when you were a kid?

RESOURCES FOR VIDEO OR **INSPIRATIONAL NEWS CLIPS**

- https://www.facebook.com/humankindvideos/
- https://www.facebook.com/lovewhatreallymatters/
- https://www.facebook.com/FamilySharecom/

ENDNOTES

Chapter 1: Why Social Media?
1. "Vince Lombardi Quotes." BrainyQuote. https://brainyquote.com/quotes/quotes/v/vincelomba38570.html

Chapter 4
1. Vaynerchuk, Gary. *Jab, Jab, Jab, Right Hook: How to Tell Your Story in a Noisy Social World.* (HarperBusiness; First edition; published November 26, 2013). Kindle edition.

Chapter 5: Ten Tips to Develop Killer Posts That Increase Engagement
1. Tom Ziglar, "If You Aim at Nothing . . ." *Ziglar*. June 2, 2016. https://ziglar.com/atiles/if-you-aim-at-nothing-2/
2. Sweet, Leonard, and Frank Viola. Jesus Manifesto. Bruchsal: GloryWorld-Medien, 2012.

Chapter 11: Three Tricks to Gain Momentum
1. https://digiday.com/marketing/get-drones-eye-view-ge-facilities-periscope/

Electric Moon Publishing, LLC is an author-friendly, custom publishing place.
EMoon collaborates with indie authors, ministries, organizations, and businesses in writing, editing, custom covers, specialty layouts, print, distribution, and marketing.

Visit us at www.emoonpublishing.com
or contact us directly at info@emoonpublishing.com.

www.ingramcontent.com/pod-product-compliance
Lightning Source LLC
Chambersburg PA
CBHW070448050426
42451CB00015B/3398